Oscar Wilde

Epigrams & Aphorisms

CLASSIC PAGES

Wilde, Oscar

Epigrams & Aphorisms

Reihe: *classic pages*

ISBN/EAN: 978-3-86741-337-4
First published in 2010 by Europaeischer Hochschulverlag GmbH & Co KG, Bremen, Germany.

© Europaeischer Hochschulverlag GmbH & Co KG, Fahrenheitstr. 1, D-28359 Bremen (www.ehv-online.com). All rights reserved.

Cover picture: Detail from an illustration of Aubrey Beardsley

This book is a reproduction of an out of print title and has originally been published by John W. Luce, Boston in 1905. Because no electronic master copies of this title could be obtained, the publisher had to reuse old copies of the text. We therefore apologize for any possible loss in quality.

Oscar Wilde

Epigrams & Aphorisms

EPIGRAMS & APHORISMS
BY OSCAR WILDE

1905: JOHN W. LUCE
AND COMPANY, BOSTON

"THE book of life begins with a man and a woman in a garden. It ends with Revelations."

Selected from

The Picture of Dorian Grey

An Ideal Husband

Lady Windemere's Fan

The Importance of Being Earnest

A Woman of No Importance

Phrases and Philosophies for the Use of the Young

Oscariana

The Canterville Ghost

The Decay of Lying

The Soul of Man under Socialism

The Critic as Artist

The Credo

L'Envoi

The English Renaissance of Art

INTRODUCTION

AN epigram is the sublimate of genius. It is a crystallization from the commonplace.

In its earliest form, indeed, it was but a mere writing upon a wall, but the modern epigram is distinguished by its particular brilliancy. It embodies the very quintessence of the thoughts of the writer. The early Greek epigram did not aim at wit, or necessarily produce the feeling of surprise, which are essential characteristics of the modern one. The writer to-day who follows the Greek epigrammatist succeeds only in being dull.

Chief among our English epigrammatists of modern days is that picturesque figure, Oscar O'Flahertie Wills Wilde. The London Athenæum, indeed, spoke of him as one whose writings would soon be found only on the shelves of the collector of the merely curious. But the Athenæum, like the great public it represents, notoriously modifies its opinions. What Mr. Wilde wrote is subject, not now, but hereafter, to final judgment, when we have reached the right point from which to observe it. A literary work, like sculpture, needs a proper perspective.

INTRODUCTION

Whatever may be thought of the writings of Oscar Wilde as a whole, it is certain that in his epigrams and aphorisms we have the very flower and blossom of his genius. Just as Rochefoucauld put together the best of his own ideas and adaptations of the thoughts of the ancients in his "Maxims"; as Franklin voiced the practical wisdom of his time in the sayings of "Poor Richard"; as Chateaubriand established for Joubert permanent fame in the "Pensées," so in this compilation the literary genius of Oscar Wilde is revealed as in no other way, and we may trace, through his writings, the gradual evolution from palpable insincerity and striving for effect, to conscious truth and literary expression for the sake of the idea conveyed rather than for the expression's sake. Flippancy, lightness of touch, dilettantism, were, after all, only masks worn for the time, although the wearer himself was conscious only of the impression created by the mask, forgetting there was, nevertheless, something behind the mask which gave it the appearance of life. Under the insouciance there was something real, something tangible — a message conveyed to those who were capable of receiving it, although in this strenuous life of the Twentieth Century, nine-tenths of the world receives its messages only over the tape of the stock market.

INTRODUCTION

It is a thankless task, in a sordid age, to preach the gospel of beauty. It is like trying to describe the coloring of an orchid to a sightless child. Perhaps it may not fully accord with the ideas of the æsthetes of whom Mr. Wilde was the recognized head to speak of a gospel of beauty, for it was one of his favorite apothegms that "Beauty cannot be taught; only revealed." We may question, although not with the ribald levity of the heavily-humorous editor of Punch, *whether the most conspicuous figure in the æsthetic movement in England was sincere or speaking merely for effect. But that there was an undercurrent of sincerity as well as cleverness in his writings, and in the school which he represented, is not to be doubted for a moment by one who is sincere. When he said that "to disagree with three-fourths of England on all points is one of the first elements of sanity," he knew the penalty he was to pay, but he did not shrink from it. He himself possessed those three things which he said the English public would never forgive in the Pre-Raphaelites — youth, power, and enthusiasm. And the English public, sometimes in good-natured fun, as with the* Archibald Grosvenor *of "Patience," and sometimes in the bitterest of malice, as with the* Lambert Streyke *of "The Colonel," proceeded to attack Mr. Wilde with ridicule. The Boston public,* represented by shallow-pated students who revealed a lack of good-breeding by insulting him on the lecture platform, took its cue from these detractors. Yet there were those who saw the thing as it was, and while they doubted the good-faith of the æsthetic leader, they saw that there was something more than superficiality in this recrudescence of Pre-Raphaelitism. For the fact remains, that in spite of the exuberant word-painting of Mr. Wilde and his tendency to lackadaisical expression in his earlier writings, his genius is undeniable, and the brilliancy which flashes out from page after page of his poems and dramas is that of the diamond, and no fading fire of a literary will-o'-the-wisp. The only form of literary expression which cannot be silenced by ridicule is that which covers a vital truth; and the fact that Mr. Wilde's work is better appreciated to-day than when it was written is the surest proof that it embodies such truth.

It was the æsthetic movement led by him that gave a new impulse to the recognition of the separate realm of the imagination. The poet does not always express his own ideas or his own emotions, and there was much in the movement itself which is no reflection of Mr. Wilde's ideas, but of that unerring sense of beauty which characterized Keats, and of which we find something in Swinburne. As an *outcome of that movement we have been brought to recognize that many of our houses are unbeautiful, our furniture is inartistic, our models of design are not the best, and that a noble drama is impossible without a noble public. These are not new things, but it takes a long time to learn some old things. In impressing these truths upon the public Mr. Wilde performed a public service. No reader of "The English Renaissance of Art" can fail to be impressed by the fact that there is something besides verbal cleverness in it; it contains those germs of truth which instantly find lodgment in a fertile mind and become themselves stimulating and creative. There is more than a mere trick in the writing of such sentences as these. There is not only the subtle play of wit, and a command of language in which the words are used to clothe the thought as rich draperies are wrapped around a beautiful figure, but there is permanent and enduring truth behind the words.*

It must be remembered by the reader that these lines were written by Mr. Wilde before he passed through the emotional "Sturm und Drang" *which is revealed in his posthumous work, and that he confesses, in that remarkable human document, that he was only amusing himself when he wrote them. But it is well known to psychologists that confessions often reveal what is not true, and others than*

Savonarola have recanted. The man who makes a confession states what he believes, in the peculiar mental condition which leads to the confession, to be true. But in another mental state he recognizes, or another may recognize, that the confession is merely an utter self-abasement. There was, undoubtedly, something of the poseur in all that Mr. Wilde published in his lifetime, and there can also be no question that in many of these epigrams he was merely aiming at an effect — he was something of a cynic, with a sneer for social conventionalities which he would replace with other conventionalities. But this spendthrift of his own genius could not escape giving utterance to truths, whatever may have been his aim. In the epigrams from "The Soul of Man Under Socialism" we find him, in spite of his confession that he was dissimulating, a thorough Republican; not a revolutionist, but a patience-preaching believer in the gospel of Democracy and the right of the people to govern themselves. Surely this was worth while. In his address in New York — doubtless the best expression which has ever been given to the doctrines of æstheticism — there is a noble, calm, clear and self-contained logic, which, whatever its purpose, is convincing. Enough that he wrote these things, and we may forgive his purpose when we recognize the lesson which they contain for art and literature and the drama in America.

It is good to know good work, as well as to do good work. In this country, at least, the name of Oscar Wilde is known to thousands who have not read his books or seen his plays — books and plays which have been ignored by some because they defied convention, by others because they were "too busy," a synonym, in many cases, for mental laziness. Heavy-witted people who cannot understand that the rapier, in the hands of a master, is quite as effective a weapon as a bludgeon, have ignored these writings altogether. Yet the work of this master of modern epigram is deserving of attention, not only for its literary form and the message it conveys to the receptive intellect, but because it is an audacious manifestation of a peculiar genius. Out of these writings has been picked a handful of gems which show the author as an artist and which must surely lead to a better comprehension of his genius. Accepting his posthumous confession, it is possible to reverse the dictum of the head of this æsthetic school, and postulate that if "It is with the best intentions that the worst work is done," good work may also be done with the worst intentions.

Boston, April, 1905.   *GEORGE HENRY SARGENT.*

The Picture of Dorian Grey

I

THERE is only one thing in the world worse than being talked about, and that is not being talked about.

Young men want to be faithful and are not, old men want to be faithless and cannot.

Punctuality is the thief of time.

One should never make one's début with a scandal, one should reserve that to give interest to one's old age.

The only way a woman can ever reform a man is by boring him so completely that he loses all possible interest in life.

With an evening coat and a white tie, even a stock broker can gain a reputation for being civilized.

Epigrams & Aphorisms

One can always be kind to people one cares nothing about.

Men marry because they are tired, women because they are curious; both are disappointed.

Conscience and cowardice are really the same things. Conscience is the trade-name of the firm.

Laughter is not a bad beginning for a friendship, and it is the best ending for one.

I choose my friends for their good looks, my acquaintances for their characters, and my enemies for their brains.

The value of an idea has nothing whatever to do with the sincerity of the man who expresses it.

It is only the intellectually lost who ever argue.

To become the spectator of one's own life is to escape the suffering of life.

The Picture of Dorian Grey

People who love once in their lives are really shallow people. What they call their loyalty and their fidelity is either the lethargy of custom or lack of imagination. Faithfulness is to the emotional life what constancy is to the intellectual life, simply a confession of failure.

Poets know how useful passion is for publication. Nowadays a broken heart will run to many editions.

Genius lasts longer than Beauty. That accounts for the fact that we all take such pains to over-educate ourselves.

Women have no appreciation of good looks. At least, good women have not.

There is no such thing as good influence. All influence is immoral—immoral from the scientific point of view.

Nothing can cure the soul but the senses, just as nothing can cure senses but the soul.

Epigrams & Aphorisms

When one is in love one begins by deceiving oneself, one ends by deceiving others. That is what the world calls romance.

There is something infinitely mean about other people's tragedies.

Women are charmingly artificial, but they have no sense of art.

We live in an age when only unnecessary things are absolutely necessary to us.

Experience is of no ethical value, it is simply the name we give our mistakes. It demonstrates that the future will be the same as the past.

Anybody can be good in the country. There are no temptations there. That is the reason why people who live out of town are so uncivilized. There are only two ways of becoming civilized. One is by being cultured, the other is by being corrupt. Country people have no opportunity of being either, so they stagnate.

The Picture of Dorian Grey

The fatality of good resolutions is that they are always too late.

There is luxury in self-reproach. When we blame ourselves we feel no one else has a right to blame us.

The worst of having a romance is that it leaves one so unromantic.

When a woman finds out that her husband is absolutely indifferent to her she either becomes dreadfully dowdy or wears very smart bonnets that some other woman's husband has to pay for.

Beauty is a form of Genius — is higher indeed, than Genius, as it needs no explanation. People say sometimes that Beauty is only superficial, but at least it is not so superficial as thought. It is only shallow people who do not judge by appearances.

The commonest thing is delightful if one only hides it.

Epigrams & Aphorisms

The one charm of marriage is that it makes a life of deception necessary for both parties.

I can believe anything, provided it is incredible.

Good artists give everything to their art and consequently are perfectly uninteresting themselves.

When we think that we are experimenting on others, we are really experimenting on ourselves.

Those who are faithful know the pleasures of love; it is the faithful who know love's tragedies.

Never trust a woman who wears mauve or a woman over thirty-five who is fond of pink ribbons. It means they have a history.

It is personality not principles that move the age.

Whenever a man does a thoroughly stupid thing it is always from the noblest motive.

The Picture of Dorian Grey

There is hardly a person in the House of Commons worth painting, though many of them would be better for a little whitewashing.

The reason we all like to think so well of others is that we are all afraid of ourselves. The basis of optimism is sheer terror.

A cigarette is the perfect type of pleasure; it is exquisite and leaves one unsatisfied.

There are only two kinds of people who are really fascinating: people who know everything, and people who know nothing.

The secret of remaining young is never to have an emotion that is unbecoming.

There is always something ridiculous about the passions of people whom one has ceased to love.

Fashion is that by which the fantastic becomes for a moment universal.

Epigrams & Aphorisms

Civilized society feels that manners are of more important than morals, and the highest respectability is of less value than the possession of a good chef. Even the cardinal virtues cannot atone for cold entrées, nor an irreproachable private life for a bad dinner and poor wines.

Insincerity is merely a method by which we can multiply our personalities.

Real beauty ends where an intellectual expression begins. Intellect is in itself an exaggeration and destroys the harmony of any face. The moment one sits down to think one becomes all nose or all forehead, or something horrid.

Being natural is simply a pose.

A man cannot be too careful in the choice of his enemies.

I can't help detesting my relations. I suppose it comes from the fact that we can't stand other people having the same faults as ourselves.

The Picture of Dorian Grey

We live in an age that reads too much to be wise and thinks too much to be beautiful.

Nothing makes one so vain as being told that one is a sinner.

In good society, taking some one's else admirer when one loses one's own always whitewashes a woman.

Good resolutions are a useless attempt to interfere with scientific laws; their origin pure vanity, their results absolutely nil.

One should absorb the color of life, but one should never remember its details.

The charm of the past is that it is past, but women never know when the curtain has fallen. They always want a sixth act.

Death and vulgarity are the only two facts in the nineteenth century that one cannot explain away.

Epigrams & Aphorisms

It is an odd thing, but every one who disappears is said to be seen in San Francisco. It must be a delightful city and possess all the attractions of the next world.

One can never pay too high a price for any sensation.

To test the Reality we must see it on the tight rope. When the verities become acrobats we can judge them.

The costume of the nineteenth century is detestable. Sin is the only real color-element left in modern life.

I can stand brute force, but brute reason is quite unbearable. There is something unfair about its use. It is hitting below the intellect.

It is better to be beautiful than to be good, but it is better to be good than to be ugly.

The tragedy of old age is not that one is old, but that one is young.

The Picture of Dorian Grey

Only sentimentalists can repeat an emotion.

No woman is a genius: women are a decorative sex. They never have anything to say, but they say it charmingly. They represent the triumph of matter over mind, just as men represent the triumph of mind over morals. There are only two kinds of women, the plain and the colored. The plain women are very useful. If you want to gain a reputation for respectability you have merely to take them down to supper. The other women are very charming. They commit one mistake, however. They paint in order to try to look young. Our grandmothers painted in order to try to talk brilliantly. Rouge and esprit used to go together. That has all gone out now. As long as a woman can look ten years younger than her own daughter she is perfectly satisfied.

It is simply expression that gives reality to things.

The only difference between a caprice and a lifelong passion is that caprice lasts a little longer.

Epigrams & Aphorisms

I like Wagner's music better than any other music. It is so loud that one can talk the whole time without people hearing what one says. That is a great advantage.

The mind of a thoroughly well-informed man is like a bric-à-brac shop, all monsters and dust and everything priced above its proper value.

If one hears bad music it is one's duty to drown it by one's conversation.

Always! that is a dreadful word. Women are so fond of using it. They spoil every romance by trying to make it last forever.

Tea is the only simple pleasure left to us.

It is only shallow people who require years to get rid of an emotion. A man who is master of himself can end a sorrow as easily as he can invent a pleasure.

An Ideal Husband

II

Morality is simply the attitude we adopt toward people whom we personally dislike.

Modern women find a new scandal as becoming as a new bonnet, and air them both in the Park every afternoon.

Musical people are so absurdly unreasonable. They always want one to be perfectly dumb at the very moment when one is longing to be absolutely deaf.

Nothing is so dangerous as being too modern; one is apt to grow old fashioned quite suddenly.

Nothing ages women so rapidly as having married the general rule.

Vulgarity is simply the conduct of other people, just as falsehoods are the truths of other people.

Epigrams & Aphorisms

To expect the unexpected shows a thoroughly modern intellect.

No woman, plain or pretty, has any common-sense at all. Common-sense is the privilege of our sex and we men are so self-sacrificing that we never use it.

Spies are of no use nowadays. Their profession is over. The newspapers do their work instead.

One should always play fairly when one has the winning cards.

An acquaintance that begins with a compliment is sure to develop into a real friendship.

Optimism begins in a broad grin, and Pessimism ends with blue spectacles. Both are merely poses.

Romance should never begin with sentiment. It should begin with science and end with a settlement.

An Ideal Husband

When a man has once loved a woman he will do anything for her except continue to love her.

Philanthropy is the refuge of people who wish to annoy their fellow-creatures.

The London season is entirely matrimonial. People are either hunting for husbands or hiding from them.

Society has gone to the dogs: a lot of nobodies talking about nothing.

Pleasure is the only thing to live for. Nothing ages like happiness.

There is only one real tragedy in a woman's life. The fact that her past is always her lover, and her future invariably her husband.

A woman whose size in gloves is seven and three quarters never knows much about anything.

Questions are never indiscreet, answers sometimes are.

Epigrams & Aphorisms

Political parties are the only places left to us where people don't talk politics.

A man who allows himself to be convinced by an argument is a thoroughly unreasonable person, which accounts for so much in women that their husbands never appreciate in them.

Only dull people are brilliant at breakfast.

In modern life nothing produces such an effect as a good platitude. It makes the whole world kin.

Secrets from other people's wives are a necessary luxury in modern life, but no man should have a secret from his own wife. She invariably finds out. Women have a wonderful instinct about things. They can discover everything except the obvious.

If one could only teach the English how to talk and the Irish how to listen society would be quite civilized.

An Ideal Husband

The only thing to do with good advice is to pass it on. It is never of any use to oneself.

London society is entirely composed of beautiful idiots and brilliant lunatics.

The only possible society is oneself.

In the case of a very fascinating woman, sex is a challenge, not a defense.

Women are never disarmed by compliments, men always are.

Self-sacrifice is a thing that should be put down by law. It is so demoralizing to the people for whom one sacrifices oneself.

Pluck is not so common nowadays as genius.

Science cannot grapple with the problem of women. It can never grapple with the irrational. That is why there is no future before it in this world.

Epigrams & Aphorisms

To love oneself is the beginning of a lifelong romance.

It is always nice to be expected and not to arrive.

Being educated puts one almost on a level with the commercial classes.

No man is rich enough to buy back his past.

One's past is what one is. It is the only thing by which people should be judged.

The reason we are so pleased to find out other people's secrets is that it distracts public attention from our own.

Woman's first duty in life is to her dressmaker. What the second duty is no one has yet discovered.

Fashion is what one wears oneself. What is unfashionable is what other people wear.

Youth isn't an affectation. Youth is an art.

An Ideal Husband

Modern women understand everything except their husbands.

Fathers should be neither seen nor heard. That is the only proper basis for family life.

Lady Windemere's Fan

III

We are all of us so hard-up nowadays that the only pleasant things to pay are compliments. They're the only things we can pay.

If you pretend to be good, the world takes you very seriously. If you pretend to be bad, it doesn't. Such is the astounding stupidity of optimism.

I can resist everything except temptation.

It is a curious thing about the game of marriage — a game, by the way, that is going out of fashion — the wives hold all the honors and invariably lose the odd trick.

A heart doesn't go with modern dress. It makes one look old.

Nowadays to be intelligible is to be found out.

Epigrams & Aphorisms

A cynic is a man who knows the price of everything, and the value of nothing.

A sentimentalist is a man who sees an absurd value in everything and doesn't know the market price of a single thing.

The world is packed with good women. To know them is a middle-class education.

Life is far too important a thing ever to talk seriously about.

Women always want one to be good. And if we are good when they meet us, they don't love us at all. They like to find us quite irretrievably bad and to leave us quite unattractively good.

What consoles one nowadays is not repentance, but pleasure. Repentance is quite out of date, and beside, if a woman really repents, she has to go to a bad dressmaker, otherwise no one believes in her.

Lady Windemere's Fan

We are all in the gutter, but some of us are looking at the stars.

Experience is a question of instinct about life.

Actions are the first tragedies in life, words are the second. Words are perhaps the worst. Words are merciless.

Ideals are dangerous things. Realities wound, but they are better.

There is nothing in the world like the devotion of a married woman. It is a thing no married man knows anything about.

In this world there are only two tragedies. One is not getting what one wants, and the other is getting it. The last is much the worst; the last is a real tragedy!

Misfortunes one can endure — they come from outside, they are accidents. But to suffer for one's own faults — Ah! there is the sting of life.

Epigrams & Aphorisms

One can always recognize women who trust their husbands, they look so thoroughly unhappy.

Good people do a great deal of harm in the world. Certainly the greatest harm they do is that they make badness of such extraordinary importance. It is absurd to divide people into good and bad. People are either charming or tedious.

Men may become old, but they never become good.

My experience is that as soon as people are old enough to know better, they don't know anything at all.

It takes a thoroughly good woman to do a thoroughly stupid thing.

Nothing looks so like innocence as an indiscretion.

Crying is the refuge of plain women but the ruin of pretty ones.

Lady Windemere's Fan

Men are such cowards. They outrage every law of the world, and are afraid of the world's tongue.

It is an awfully dangerous thing to come across a woman who thoroughly understands one. They always end by marrying one.

The youth of the present day are quite monstrous. They have absolutely no respect for dyed hair.

History is merely gossip. But scandal is gossip made tedious by morality. A man who moralizes is usually a hypocrite, and a woman who moralizes is invariably plain. There is nothing in the world as unbecoming to a woman as a Nonconformist conscience.

A mother who doesn't part with a daughter every season has no real affection.

The world has grown suspicious of anything that looks like a happy married life.

Epigrams & Aphorisms

It is most dangerous nowadays for a husband to pay any attention to his wife in public. It always makes people think that he beats her when they are alone.

Nature's gentlemen are the worst type of gentlemen I know.

Even business should have a picturesque background. With a proper back-ground a woman can do anything.

When men give up saying what is charming, they cease thinking what is charming.

My own business always bores me to death, I prefer other people's.

Wicked women bother one, good women bore one. That is the only difference between them.

How marriage ruins a man! It is as demoralizing as cigarettes, and far more expensive.

The
Importance of Being Earnest

IV

The truth is rarely pure and never simple. Modern life would be very tedious if it were either, and modern literature an impossibility.

The amount of women who flirt with their own husbands is scandalous. It is simply washing one's clean linen in public.

The modern sympathy with invalids is morbid. Illness of any kind is hardly a thing to be encouraged in others.

A man who desires to get married should know either everything or nothing.

Ignorance is like a delicate exotic fruit; touch it and the bloom is gone. Fortunately, in England at any rate, Education produces no effect whatsoever.

Epigrams & Aphorisms

Relations are simply a tedious pack of people who haven't got the remotest knowledge of how to live, nor the smallest instinct about when to die.

The way to behave to a woman is to make love to her if she is pretty, and to some one else if she is plain.

Women only call each other sister after they have called each other a lot of other things first.

Memory is the diary that chronicles things that never have happened and couldn't possibly have happened.

The good end happily, the bad unhappily. That is what fiction means.

The two weak points of our age are want of principle and want of profile. Style depends largely on the way the chin is worn. They are worn very high at present.

Divorces are made in heaven.

The Importance of Being Earnest

Long engagements give people the opportunity of finding out each other's character before marriage, which is never advisable.

No woman should ever be quite accurate about her age. It looks so calculating.

Arguments are to be avoided; they are always vulgar and often convincing.

Never speak disrespectfully of society. Only people who can't get into it do that.

Girls never marry the men they flirt with. Girls don't think it right.

It is absurd to have a hard and fast rule about what one should read and what one shouldn't. More than half of modern culture depends on what one shouldn't read.

It is important not to keep a business engagement if one wants to retain any sense of the beauty of life.

Epigrams & Aphorisms

If one plays good music people don't listen, and if one plays bad music people don't talk.

What with the duties expected of one during one's lifetime, and the duties exacted from one after one's death, land has ceased to be either a profit or pleasure. It gives one position and prevents one from keeping it up.

By persistently remaining single a man converts himself into a permanent public temptation.

One's duty as a gentleman should never interfere with one's pleasures in the slightest degree.

One must be serious about something if one wants to have any amusement in life.

An engagement is hardly a serious one that has not been broken off at least once.

The only way to atone for being occasionally over-dressed is by being always absolutely over-educated.

The Importance of Being Earnest

Whenever one has anything unpleasant to say one should always be quite candid.

Flowers are as common in the country as people are in London.

It is very vulgar to talk about one's own business. Only people like stock-brokers do that, and then merely at dinner parties.

Hesitation of any kind is a sign of mental decay in the young, of physical weakness in the old.

Three addresses always inspire confidence — even in tradesmen.

All women become like their mothers — that is their tragedy. No man does. That's his.

Few parents nowadays pay any regard to what their children say to them. The old-fashioned respect for the young is fast dying out.

In married life three is company and two is none.

A Woman of No Importance

V

Twenty years of romance make a woman look like a ruin, but twenty years of marriage make her something like a public building.

To have the reputation of possessing the most perfect social tact, talk to every woman as if you loved her, and to every man as if he bored you.

To get into the best society nowadays, one has either to feed people, amuse people, or shock people.

Women are pictures, men are problems: if you want to know what a woman really means, look at her, don't listen to her.

There is no such thing as romance in our day, women have become too brilliant; nothing spoils a romance so much as a sense of humor in the woman.

Epigrams & Aphorisms

Children begin by loving their parents; after a time they judge them, rarely, if ever, do they forgive them.

If a man is a gentleman he knows quite enough, and if he is not a gentleman whatever he knows is bad for him.

Discontent is the first step in the progress of a man or a nation.

Sentiment is all very well for a boutonnière, but a well-tied tie is the first serious step in life.

Clever people never listen and stupid people never talk.

The youth of America is their oldest tradition. It has been going on now for three hundred years. To hear them talk one would imagine they were in their first childhood. As far as civilization goes they are in their second.

Nowadays it is only the unreadable that occurs.

A Woman of No Importance

Women have become so highly educated that nothing should surprise them except happy marriages.

Health — the silliest word in our language, and one knows the popular idea of health. The English country gentleman galloping after a fox — the unspeakable in full pursuit of the uneatable.

It is safer to believe evil of everyone until people are found out to be good, but that requires a great deal of investigation nowadays.

The basis of every scandal is an absolutely immoral certainty.

Plain women are always jealous of their husbands, beautiful women never are; they have no time, they are always so occupied in being jealous of other people's husbands.

A bad man is the sort of man who admires innocence.

Epigrams & Aphorisms

A bad woman is the sort of woman a man never gets tired of.

It is perfectly monstrous the way people go about nowadays saying things against one, behind one's back, that are absolutely and entirely true.

America is a Paradise for women — that is why, like Eve, the American women are extremely anxious to get out of it.

To elope is cowardly; it is running away from danger; and danger has become so rare in modern life.

The one advantage of playing with fire is that one never even gets singed. It is the people who don't know how to play with it that get burned up.

There is no objection to plain women being Puritans; it is the only excuse they have for being plain.

A Woman of No Importance

Women as a sex are Sphinxes without secrets.

The Soul is born old, but it grows young; that is the comedy of life. The Body is born young and grows old; that is Life's tragedy.

Vulgar habit people have nowadays of asking one, after one has given them an idea, whether one is serious or not. Nothing is serious except passion. The intellect is an instrument on which one plays, that is all. The only serious form of intellect is the British intellect. And on the British form of intellect the illiterates play the drum.

All Americans dress well — they get their clothes in Paris.

It is absurd to say that there are neither ruins nor curiosities in America when they have their mothers and their manners.

After a good dinner one could forgive anybody, even one's own relations.

Epigrams & Aphorisms

Men are horribly tedious when they are good husbands, and abominably conceited when they are not.

Men always want to be a woman's first love — women like to be a man's last romance.

Women are a fascinatingly wilful set. Every woman is a rebel and usually in wild revolt against herself.

All men are married women's property; that is the only true definition of what married women's property really is.

One can survive everything except Death, and live down everything except a good reputation.

Society is a necessary thing. No man has any real success in this world unless he has women to back him, and women rule society. If you have not got women on your side you are quite over. You might as well be a barrister, or a stock-broker, or a journalist at once.

A Woman of No Importance

The history of woman is the history of the worst form of tryanny the world has ever known: the tyranny of the weak over the strong. It is the only tyranny that lasts.

Simple pleasures are the last refuge of the complex.

One should sympathize with the joy, the beauty, the color of life — the less said about life's sores the better.

Women have always been picturesque protests against the mere existence of common sense.

When good Americans die they go to Paris, when bad Americans die they go to America.

When a man is old enough to do wrong he should be old enough to do right also.

When one has never heard a man's name in the course of one's life it speaks volumes for him; he must be quite respectable.

Epigrams & Aphorisms

Duty is what one expects from others — it is not what one does oneself.

English women conceal their feelings until after they are married, then they show them.

One should never trust a woman who tells one her real age. A woman who would tell that would tell anything.

One should never take sides in anything — taking sides is the beginning of sincerity, and earnestness follows shortly after, and the human being becomes a bore.

The happiness of a married man depends on the people he has not married.

One should always be in love: that is the reason one should never marry.

The only difference between a saint and a sinner is that every saint has a past, and every sinner has a future.

A Woman of No Importance

The world has always laughed at its own tragedies, that being the only way in which it has been able to bear them; consequently, whatever the world has treated seriously belongs to the comedy side of things.

Women love men for their defects; if men have enough of them women will forgive them everything, even their gigantic intellects.

The secret of life is to appreciate the pleasure of being terribly deceived.

Moderation is a fatal thing; nothing succeeds like excess.

Memory in a woman is the beginning of dowdiness.

When a man says he has exhausted life one always knows life has exhausted him.

Men know life too early, women know life too late.

Epigrams & Aphorisms

The world is divided into two classes, those who believe the incredible, and those who do the improbable.

All thought is immoral. Its very essence is destruction. If you think of anything you kill it. Nothing survives being thought of.

Women have a much better time than men in this world; there are far more things forbidden to them.

To be in society is merely a bore, but to be out of it simply a tragedy.

There is nothing like youth. The middle aged are mortgaged to Life. The old are in Life's lumber-room. But youth is the Lord of Life. Youth has a kingdom waiting for it. Every one is born a king, and most people die in exile, like most kings.

American women are wonderfully clever in concealing their parents.

A Woman of No Importance

A really *grande passion* is comparatively rare nowadays. It is the privilege of people who have nothing to do. That is the only use of the idle classes in the country.

More marriages are ruined nowadays by the common sense of the husband than by anything else. How can a woman be expected to be happy with a man who insists on treating her as if she were a perfectly rational being.

A husband is a sort of promissory note — a woman is tired of meeting him.

Life is a *mauvais quart d'heure* made up of exquisite moments.

Phrases and Philosophies for the Use of the Young

VI

The first duty in life is to be as artificial as possible. What the second duty is no one has yet discovered.

Wickedness is a myth invented by good people to account for the curious attractiveness of others.

Those who see any difference between soul and body have neither.

Religions die when they are proved to be true. Science is the record of dead religions.

The well bred contradict other people. The wise contradict themselves.

Nothing that actually occurs is of the smallest importance.

Dulness is the coming of age of seriousness.

Epigrams & Aphorisms

If one tells the truth, one is sure, sooner or later, to be found out.

In all unimportant matters style not sincerity is the essential. In all important matters style not sincerity is the essential.

It is only by not paying our bills that we can hope to live in the memory of the commercial classes.

Only the shallow know themselves.

Time is waste of money.

There is a fatality about all good resolutions. They are invariably made too soon.

Any preoccupation with ideas of what is right or wrong in conduct shows an arrested intellectual development.

A truth ceases to be true when more than one person believes in it.

Phrases and Philosophies

The vanishing point of social tolerance is represented by a woman without sentiment enough to yearn for love in a cottage, and without sense enough to refuse it.

Ambition is the last refuge of the failure.

One should either be a work of art, or wear a work of art.

It is only the superficial qualities that last. Man's deeper nature is soon found out.

Industry is the root of all ugliness.

The old believe everything; the middle aged suspect everything; the young know everything.

The condition of perfection is idleness; the aim of perfection is youth.

Modern morality consists in accepting the standard of one's age.

Women give to men the very gold of their lives, but they invariably want it back in very small change.

Oscariana

VII

The costume of the nineteenth century is detestable. Sin is the only real color element left in modern life.

Evening clothes on a London merchant remind one of a morocco binding on a cook-book or a doyly on a stove lid.

Credit is the capital of a younger son, and he can live charmingly on it.

To get back one's youth one has merely to repeat one's follies.

Nowadays most people die of a sort of creeping common sense, and discover, when it is too late, that the only thing one never regrets are one's mistakes.

No civilized man ever regrets a pleasure, and no uncivilized man ever knows what a pleasure is.

Epigrams & Aphorisms

If a man treats life artistically, his brain is in his heart.

Pleasure is nature's test, her sign of approval. When we are happy we are always good; but when we are good we are not always happy.

Most people become bankrupt through having invested too heavily in the prose of life. To have ruined oneself over poetry is an honor.

Being adored is a nuisance. Women treat us just as Humanity treats its gods. They worship us, and are always bothering us to do something for them.

The only horrible thing in the world is ennui. That is the one sin for which there is no forgiveness.

There is no such thing as an omen. Destiny does not send us heralds. She is too wise or too cruel for that.

Oscariana

How fond women are of doing dangerous things. It is one of the qualities in them that I admire most. A woman will flirt with anybody in the world as long as other people are looking on.

A Radical is merely a man who is never dined, and a Tory simply a gentleman who has never thought.

The world has been made by fools that wise men may live in it.

The Canterville Ghost

VIII

The subjects discussed were merely such as form the ordinary conversation of cultured Americans of the better class, such as the immense superiority of Miss Fanny Davenport over Sara Bernhardt as an actress; the difficulty of obtaining green corn, buckwheat cakes and hominy, even in the best English houses; the importance of Boston in the development of the world-soul; the advantages of the baggage-check system in railway traveling; and the sweetness of the New York acccnt as compared to the London drawl.

The reward of all good little American girls is the coronet — if they are good enough and rich enough.

If a woman cannot make her mistakes charmingly she is merely a female.

The Decay of Lying

IX

Lying, the telling of beautiful untrue things, is the proper aim of Art.

Art reveals Nature's lack of design, her curious crudities, her absolutely unfinished condition. Nature has good intentions, but she cannot carry them out. Art is our gallant attempt to teach Nature her proper place.

The crude commercialism of America, its materializing spirit, its indifference to the poetical side of things, its lack of imagination and of high unattainable ideals, are entirely due to that country having adopted for its national hero one who, according to his own confession, was incapable of telling a lie; and it is not too much to say that the story of George Washington and the cherry tree has done more harm, and in a shorter space of time, than any other moral tale in the whole of literature.

Epigrams & Aphorisms

The aim of the liar is simply to charm, to delight, to give pleasure. He is the very basis of civilized society.

Life imitates Art far more than Art imitates Life.

Literature always anticipates life. It does not copy it, but molds it to its purpose.

No great artist ever sees things as they really are. If he did, he would cease to be an artist.

Most of our modern portrait painters are doomed to absolute oblivion. They never paint what they see. They paint what the public sees, and the public never sees anything.

At twilight nature becomes a wonderfully suggestive effect, and is not without loveliness, though perhaps its chief use is to illustrate quotations from the poets.

England is the home of lost ideas.

The Decay of Lying

Nature hates Mind. Thinking is the most unhealthy thing in the world, and people die of it just as they die of any other disease. Fortunately, in England at any rate, thought is not catching. Our splendid physique is entirely due to our national stupidity.

People are beginning to be over-educated; at least everybody who is incapable of learning has taken to teaching.

If a man is sufficiently unimaginative to produce evidence in support of a lie, he might just as well speak the truth at once.

What is interesting about people in good society is the mask that each one of them wears, not the reality that lies behind the mask.

We are a degraded race and have sold our birthright for a mess of facts.

Nature is always behind the age.

Epigrams & Aphorisms

Many a young man starts in life with a natural gift of exaggeration which, if nurtured in congenial and sympathetic surroundings, might grow into something really great and wonderful. But, as a rule, he comes to nothing. He either falls into careless habits of accuracy, or takes to frequenting the society of the aged and well-informed. Both things are equally fatal to his imagination, as indeed they would be fatal to the imagination of anybody, and in a short time he develops a morbid and unhealthy faculty of truth telling, begins to verify all statements made in his presence, has no hesitation in contradicting people who are much younger than himself, and often ends by writing novels which are so like life that no one can possibly believe in their probability.

Lying for the sake of the improvement of the young, which is the basis of home education, still lingers among us, but the only form of lying that is absolutely beyond reproach is lying for its own sake, and the highest development of this is, lying in art.

The Decay of Lying

One touch of Nature may make the whole world kin, but two touches of Nature will destroy any work of art.

All bad art comes from returning to Life and Nature and elevating them into ideals. Life and Nature may sometimes be used as part of Art's rough material, but before they are of any real service to Art they must be translated into artistic conventions.

The only beautiful things are the things that do not concern us.

Nobody of any real culture ever talks nowadays about the beauty of the sunset. Sunsets are quite old fashioned.

The Soul of Man Under Socialism

X

There are three kinds of despots. There is the despot who tyrannizes over the body. There is the despot who tyrannizes over the soul. There is the despot who tyrannizes over the soul and body alike. The first is called the Prince. The second is called the Pope. The third is called the People.

There is not a single real poet or prose writer of this century on whom the British public have not solemnly conferred diplomas of immorality, and these diplomas practically take the place with us, of what in France is the formal recognition of an Academy of Letters, and fortunately make the establishment of such an institution quite unnecessary in England.

It is immoral to use private property in order to alleviate the horrible evils that result from the institution of private property.

Epigrams & Aphorisms

Evolution is the law of life, and there is no evolution save toward Individualism.

Selfishness is not living as one wishes to live. It is asking others to live as one wishes to live.

In America the President reigns for four years, and Journalism governs forever and ever. Fortunately, in America, Journalism has carried its authority to the grossest and most brutal extreme. It is no longer seriously treated.

In centuries before ours the public nailed the ears of journalists to the pump. In this century journalists have nailed their own ears to the keyhole.

One who is an emperor or king may stoop down and pick up a brush for a painter, but when the democracy stoops down it is merely to throw mud.

The majority of men spoil their lives by an exaggerated and unhealthy altruism.

The Soul of Man Under Socialism

A Community is infinitely more brutalized by the habitual employment of punishment than it is by the occasional occurrence of crime.

Disobedience in the eyes of any one who has read history is man's original virtue. It is through disobedience that progress has been made, through disobedience and through rebellion.

He who would lead a Christ-like life is he who is perfectly and absolutely himself. He may be a great poet, or a great man of science, or a young student at the University, or one who watches sheep upon a moor, or a maker of dramas like Shakespeare, or a thinker about God like Spinoza, or a child who plays in a garden, or a fisherman who throws his nets into the sea. It does not matter what he is as long as he realizes the perfection of the soul that is within him.

There is only one class in the community that thinks more about money than the rich, and that is the poor. The poor can think of nothing else. That is the misery of being poor.

Epigrams & Aphorisms

Individualism does not come to a man with any claims upon him at all. It comes naturally and inevitably out of man. It is the point to which all development tends. It is the differentiation to which all organisms grow. It is the perfection that is inherent in every mode of life, and toward which every mode of life quickens. Individualism exercises no compulsion over man. On the contrary, it says to man that he should suffer no compulsion to be exercised over him. It does not try to force people to be good. It knows that people are good when they are let alone. To ask whether Individualism is practical is like asking whether Evolution is practical. Evolution is the law of life, and there is no evolution except toward individualism.

To call an artist morbid because he deals with morbidity as his subject-matter is as silly as if one called Shakespeare mad because he wrote King Lear.

As for begging, it is safer to beg than to take, but it is finer to take than to beg.

The Soul of Man Under Socialism

A map of the world that does not include Utopia is not worth even glancing at, for it leaves out the one country at which Humanity is always landing. And when Humanity lands there, it looks out, and, seeing a better country, sets sail. Progress is the realization of Utopias.

Nothing should be able to harm a man except himself. Nothing should be able to rob a man at all. What a man really has, is what is in him. What is outside of him should be a matter of no importance.

The public has always in every age been badly brought up. They are continually asking art to be popular, to please their want of taste, to flatter their absurd vanity, to show them what they ought to be tired of seeing, and to distract their thoughts when they are tired of their own stupidity. Now art should never try to be popular. The public should try to make itself artistic.

The public have an insatiable curiosity to know everything, except what is worth knowing.

Epigrams & Aphorisms

What man has sought for is neither pain or pleasure, but simply Life. Man has sought to live intensely, fully, perfectly. When he can do so without exercising restraint on others, or suffering it ever, and his activities are all pleasurable to him, he will be saner, healthier, more civilized, more himself. Pleasure is Nature's test, her sign of approval. When man is happy he is at harmony with himself and his environment.

A work of art is the unique result of a unique temperament. Its beauty comes from the fact that its author is what he is. It has nothing to do with the fact that other people want what they want. Indeed, the moment the artist takes notice of what other people want, and tries to supply the demand, he ceases to be an artist and becomes a dull or an amusing craftsman, an honest or a dishonest tradesman. Art is the most intense mode of individualism the world has known.

The Critic as Artist

XI

I dislike modern memoirs. They are generally written by people who have either entirely lost their memories, or have never done anything worth remembering; which, however, is, no doubt, the true explanation of their popularity, as the English public always feels perfectly at its ease when a mediocrity is talking to it.

The public is wonderfully tolerant. It forgives everything except genius.

Cheap editions of great books may be delightful, but cheap editions of great men are absolutely detestable.

Listening to the conversation of some one older than yourself is always a dangerous thing to do; if you allow it to degenerate to a habit, you will find it absolutely fatal to any intellectual development.

Epigrams & Aphorisms

Every great man nowadays has his disciples, and it is always Judas who writes the biography.

Learned conversation is either the affectation of the ignorant or the profession of the mentally unemployed. Improving conversation is merely the foolish method by which the still more foolish philanthropist feebly tries to disarm the just rancor of the criminal classes.

How appalling is the ignorance which is the inevitable result of the fatal habit of imparting opinions!

Just as the philanthropist is the nuisance of the ethical sphere, so the nuisance of the intellectual sphere is the man who is so occupied in trying to educate others, that he has never had any time to educate himself.

Man is a rational animal who always loses his temper when he is called upon to act in accordance with the dictates of reason.

The Critic as Artist

Truth, in matters of religion, is simply the opinion that has survived.

It is only an auctioneer who can equally and impartially admire all schools of art.

There are two ways of disliking art. One is to dislike it. The other is to like it rationally.

A little sincerity is a dangerous thing.

All bad poetry springs from genuine feeling. To be natural is to be obvious, and to be obvious is to be inartistic.

England has done one thing; it has invented and established public opinion, which is an attempt to organize the ignorance of the community, and to elevate it to the dignity of physical force.

There is only one thing worse than Injustice, and that is Justice without her sword in her hand. When Right is not Might, it is Evil.

Epigrams & Aphorisms

It is always with the best intentions that the worst work is done.

To be good according to the vulgar standard of goodness is quite easy. It merely requires a certain amount of sordid terror, a certain lack of imaginative thought, and a certain low passion for middle-class respectability.

Science is out of the reach of morals, for her eyes are fixed upon eternal truths. Art is out of the reach of morals, for her eyes are fixed upon things beautiful and immortal and ever-changing.

Though of all poses a moral pose is the most offensive, still to have a pose at all is something. It is a form of recognition of the importance of treating life from a definite and reasoned standpoint.

Life makes us pay too high a price for its wares, and we purchase the meanest of its secrets at a cost that is monstrous and infinite.

The Critic as Artist

It takes a thoroughly selfish age, like our own, to deify self-sacrifice.

Those who try to lead the people can only do so by following the mob.

Charity creates a multitude of evils.

The mere existence of conscience is a sign of our imperfect development. It must be merged in instinct before we become fine. Self-denial is simply a method by which man arrests his progress.

When man acts he is a puppet. When he describes he is a poet.

Life is terribly deficient in form. Its catastrophes happen in a wrong way and to the wrong people. There is a grotesque horror about its comedies, and its tragedies seem to culminate in farce. One is always wounded when one approaches it. Things last either too long or not long enough.

Epigrams & Aphorisms

Conversation should touch everything, but should concentrate itself on nothing.

Modern journalism justifies its own existence by the great Darwinian principle of the survival of the vulgarest.

The difference between literature and journalism is that journalism is unreadable, and literature is not read.

There is much to be said in favor of modern journalism. By giving us the opinions of the uneducated, it keeps us in touch with the ignorance of the community.

Indiscretion is the better part of valor.

The sure way of knowing nothing about life is to try to make oneself useful.

The basis of action is lack of imagination. It is the last resource of those who know not how to dream.

The Critic as Artist

He who would stir us by fiction must either give us an entirely new back-ground, or reveal to us the soul of man in its inmost workings. The first is for the moment being done for us by Mr. Rudyard Kipling. As one turns over the pages of his "Plain Tales from the Hills," one feels as if one were seated under a palm tree reading life by superb flashes of vulgarity. The mere lack of style in the story teller gives an odd journalistic realism to what he tells us. From the point of view of literature Mr. Kipling is a genius who drops his aspirates. From the point of view of life, he is a reporter who knows vulgarity better than any one has ever known it. He is our first authority on the second-rate, and has seen marvelous things through keyholes.

We live in the age of the over-worked, and the under-educated; the age in which people are so industrious that they become absolutely stupid.

To do nothing at all is the most difficult thing in the world, the most difficult and the most intellectual.

Epigrams & Aphorisms

It is to do nothing that the elect exist.

Imagination is the result of heredity. It is simply concentrated race-experience.

A dreamer is one who can only find his way by moonlight, and his punishment is that he sees the dawn before the rest of the world.

It is because Humanity has never known where it was going that it has been able to find its way.

Society often forgives the criminal; it never forgives the dreamer.

After playing Chopin, I feel as if I had been weeping over sins that I had never committed, and mourning over tragedies that were not my own. Music always seems to me to produce that effect. It creates for one a past of which one has been ignorant, and fills one with a sense of sorrows that have been hidden from one's tears.

The Critic as Artist

The meaning of any beautiful created thing is, at least, as much in the soul of him who looks at it, as it was in his soul who wrought it.

When we have fully discovered the scientific laws that govern life, we shall realize that the one person who has more illusions than the dreamer is the man of action.

Better to take pleasure in a rose than to put its root under a microscope.

The Past is of no importance. The Present is of no importance. It is with the Future that we have to deal. For the Past is what man should not have been. The Present is what man ought not to be. The Future is what artists are.

A true artist takes no notice whatever of the public. The public are to him non-existent.

Anybody can write a three-volume novel. It merely requires a complete ignorance of both life and literature.

Epigrams & Aphorisms

To know the vintage and quality of a wine one need not drink the whole cask.

It is very much more difficult to talk about a thing than to do it. In the sphere of actual life that is, of course, obvious. Anybody can make history. Only a great man can write it.

To give an accurate description of what has never occurred is the inalienable privilege and proper occupation of the historian.

Technique is really personality. That is the reason why the artist cannot teach it, why the pupil cannot learn it, and why the æsthetic critic can understand it.

Every century that produces poetry is, so far, an artificial century, and the work that seems to us to be the most natural and simple product of its time is always the result of the most self-conscious effort. There is no fine art without self-consciousness, and self-consciousness and a critical spirit are one.

The Critic as Artist

Education is an admirable thing, but it is well to remember from time to time that nothing that is worth knowing can be taught.

The Creeds are believed, not because they are rational, but because they are repeated. Yes, Form is everything. It is the secret of Life. Find expression for a sorrow and it will become dear to you. Find expression for a joy and you intensify its ecstacy. Do you wish to love? Use Love's Litany, and the words will create the yearning from which the world fancies that they spring. Have you a grief that corrodes your heart? Steep yourself in the language of grief, learn its utterance from Prince Hamlet and Queen Constance, and you will find that the mere expression is a mode of consolation, and that Form, which is the birth of Passion, is also the death of Pain. And so to return to the sphere of Art, it is Form that creates, that creates not merely the critical temperament, but also the æsthetic instinct that reveals to one all things under the condition of beauty. Start with the worship of Form, and there is no secret in Art that will not be revealed to you.

Epigrams & Aphorisms

We are born in an age when only the dull are treated seriously.

There have been critical ages that have not been creative, in the ordinary sense of the word, ages in which the spirit of man has sought to set in order the treasures of his treasure house, to separate the gold from the silver, and the silver from the lead, to count over the jewels, and to give names to the pearls. But there has never been a creative age that has not been critical also. For it is the critical faculty that invents fresh forms. The tendency of creation is to repeat itself. It is to the critical instinct that we owe each new school that springs up, each new mold that art finds ready to its hands.

A truly great artist cannot conceive of life being shown, or beauty fashioned, under any conditions other than those that he has selected. Creation employs all its critical faculty within its own sphere. It may not use it in a sphere that belongs to others. It is exactly because a man cannot do a thing that he is the proper judge of it.

The Critic as Artist

It is so easy for people to have sympathy for suffering. It is so difficult for them to have sympathy with thought. Indeed, ordinary people seem to imagine that, when they have said a theory is dangerous, they have pronounced its condemnation, whereas it is only such theories that have any true intellectual value.

The Credo

XII

To reveal art and conceal the artist is art's aim.

Those who find ugly meanings in beautiful things are corrupt without being charming.

There is no such thing as a moral or immoral book. Books are well written or badly written. That is all.

The nineteenth century dislike of Realism is the rage of Caliban at seeing his own face in the glass.

The nineteenth century dislike of romanticism is the rage of Caliban at not seeing his own face in the glass.

Diversity of opinion about a work of art shows that the work is new, complex, and vital.

Epigrams & Aphorisms

No artist has ethical sympathies. An ethical sympathy in an artist is an unpardonable mannerism of style.

From the point of view of form, the type of all the arts is the art of the musician. From the point of view of feeling, the actor's craft is the type.

We can forgive a man for making a useful thing as long as he does not admire it. The only excuse for making a useless thing is that one admires it intensely.

L'Envoi

XIII

It is not enough that a work should conform to the æsthetic demands of the age, there should be about it, if it is to give us any permanent delight, the impress of a distinct individuality. Whatever work we have in the nineteenth century must rest on the two poles of personality and perfection.

This increased sense of the absolutely satisfying value of beautiful workmanship, this recognition of the primary importance of the sensuous element in art, this love of art for art's sake, is the point in which we of the younger school have made a departure from the teaching of Mr. Ruskin — a departure definitive and different and decisive.

The English Renaissance of Art

XIV

The Origin of the Art Revolution

In the year 1847 a number of young men in London, all admirers of Keats, were in the habit of meeting together and discussing art. They had determined to revolutionize poetry and painting. To do so was to lose, in England, all their rights as citizens. They had those things which the English public never forgives — youth, power, and enthusiasm. Satire paid the usual homage which mediocrity yields to genius, blinding the British public to what is noble and beautiful, but harming the artist not at all. To disagree with three-fourths of England on all points is one of the first elements of sanity, which is a deep source of consolation in all moments of spiritual doubt.

These young men called themselves Pre-Raphaelites because, as opposed to the facile abstractions of Raphael they thought they had found a stronger realism of imagination, a more careful realism of technique, an individuality more intense.

The Sunflower and the Lily

You have heard, I think, a few of you, of two flowers connected with the æsthetic movement in England, said (I assure you erroneously) to be the food of some æsthetic young men. Well, let me tell you that the reason we love the lily and the sunflower, in spite of what Mr. Gilbert may tell you, is not for any vegetable fashion at all; it is because these two lovely flowers are in England the two most perfect models of design, the most naturally adapted for decorative art — the gaudy leonine beauty of the one and the precious loveliness of the other giving to the artist the most entire and perfect joy. And so with you; let there be no flower in your meadows that does not wreathe its tendrils around your pillows, no little leaf in your Titan forests that does not lend its form to design, no curving spray of wild rose or brier that does not live forever in carven arch or window of marble, no bird in your air that is not

The English Renaissance of Art

giving the iridescent wonder of its color, the exquisite curves of its wings in flight, to make more precious the preciousness of simple adornment; for the voices that have their dwelling in sea and mountain are not the chosen music of liberty only. Other messages are there in the wonder of wind-swept heights and the majesty of silent deep — messages that, if you will listen to them, will give you the wonder of all new imagination, the treasure of all new beauty. We spend our days, each one of us, in looking for the secret of life. Well, the secret of life is in art.

The Novel and the Drama

The novel has not killed the play, as some critics would persuade us. The romantic period of France shows that the work of Balzac and of Hugo grew up side by side together — nay, more, were complementary to each other, although neither of them saw it. The drama is the meeting-place of art and life; it deals, as Mazzini said, not merely with man, but with social man, with man in relation to God and to humanity. It is the product of a period of great national, united energy. It is impossible without a noble public, and it belongs to such ages as the age of Elizabeth at London, Pericles at Athens. It is part of such lofty, moral, and spiritual ardor as came to Greece after the defeat of the Persian fleet, and to Englishmen after the wreck of the Armada of Spain.

Shelley felt how incomplete our movement was in this respect, and has shown in one great tragedy by what terror and pity he would have pacified our age, but in spite of the "Cenci" the drama is one of the artistic forms through which the genius of England seeks in vain an outlet and an expression.

Where Morality is Not in Question

In nations, as in individuals, if the passion for creation be not accompanied by the critical, the æsthetic faculty also, it will be sure to waste its strength. It is not an increased moral sense or moral supervision that your literature needs. Indeed, one should never talk of a moral or immoral poem. Poems are either well written or badly written; that is all. Any element of morals

The English Renaissance of Art

or implied reference to a standard of good and evil in art is often a sign of a certain incompleteness of vision. All good work aims at a purely artistic effect. But as in your cities so in your literature, it is an increased sensibility to beauty that is lacking. All noble work is not national merely, but universal. Spiritual freedom your own generous lives and liberal air will give you. From us you will learn the classical restraint of form. Love art for its own sake and then all things that you need will be added to you. This devotion to beauty, and to the creation of beautiful things, is the test of all great civilizations; it is what makes the life of each citizen a sacrament, and not a speculation. For beauty is the only thing that time cannot harm. Philosophies fall away like sand, creeds follow one another, but what is beautiful is a joy for all seasons, a possession for all eternity.

⚜

America to Complete the Movement

It is rather, perhaps, to you that we would turn to complete and perfect this great movement of ours, for there is something Hellenic in your air and world, something that has a quicker breath of the joy and power of Elizabeth's England about it than our ancient civilization can give us. For you, at least, are young; no hungry generations tread you down, and the past does not mock you with the ruins of a beauty the secret of whose creation you have lost. That very absence of tradition which Ruskin thought would rob your rivers of their laughter and your flowers of their light may be rather the source of your freedom and strength. To speak in literature with the perfect rectitude of the movement of animals, and the unimpeachableness of the sentiment of trees and the grass by the roadside, has been defined by one of your poets as the flawless triumph of art; it is a triumph which you above all other nations may be destined to achieve. For the voices that have their dwelling in sea and mountain are not the chosen music of liberty only. Other messages are there, if you will but listen to them — may yield you the splendor of some new imagination, the marvel of some new liberty.